Angels and Visitors

Angels and Visitors

JEAN-MARK SENS

RESOURCE *Publications* · Eugene, Oregon

ANGELS AND VISITORS

Resource Publications
An Imprint of Wipf and Stock Publishers
199 W. 8th Ave., Suite 3
Eugene, OR 97401

www.wipfandstock.com

PAPERBACK ISBN: 978-1-6667-3764-6
HARDCOVER ISBN: 978-1-6667-9732-9
EBOOK ISBN: 978-1-6667-9733-6

MAY 31, 2022 8:17 AM

For the Glory of God, Angels, the community at Mepkin Abbey, and all those who participated in the making of these poems, and most fittingly Angela.

Many thanks to Peter Vale for his kind and judicious suggestions for the introduction.

For Angels rent the House next ours,
Wherever we remove—

EMILY DICKINSON

There hovers in that moment, wraith-like and like a
        [plume of steam an aftermath,
A still and quiet angel of knowledge and of
        [comprehension.

GEORGE OPPEN

I enable myself
By any device
An angel would recognize

Even if he came
While I was away
A good sign
Might make him stay

SAMUEL MENASHE

Do you hear
Does anyone
hear the man
repeating and repeating
himself in the snow?

MIKE WHITE

Contents

INTRODUCTION

ANGELS AND VISITORS is the product of many years of reading, praying, wondering, wrestling, writing, and refining.

I can trace its inception to my early years, when I first came across Rafael Alberti's 1929 masterpiece, *Sobre los ángeles* (*Concerning the Angels*). Alberti's angels abide in a materialism that renders them mute in spirit. As if locked in a world which they oppose rather than blissfully inhabit, pessimism abounds and threatens redemption and illumination. Indeed, and as C. M. Bowra explains in his *The Creative Experiment* (1958), Alberti's angels proceed from a disappointment in his own inability to rekindle creativity. Regardless, I have returned to his poems quite often, and they have inspired me to venture into more ecstatic and magical poetry.

More recently, I have read Peter Kreeft's *Angels and Demons: What Do We Really Know about Them?* (1995). I was, in fact, on a quest to see if my poems would resonate with orthodox Christian theology. This was not a primary concern of mine but was something I undertook more so out of curiosity. What I found was that the tenets which Kreeft explores had be functioning all along as the enlightening catalyst for my writing. Simply put, my poems flowed from a desire to encounter the sacred on the level of the life-giving *anima* ("soul").

This has not, however, limited me to the Christian realm. Indeed, angels have always cut across different religions and creeds. They have even ventured into the commercial sector, featuring on everything from the softest of toilet paper to the most sentimental of greeting cards. My desire here is to anchor them triumphantly in the spirit while evoking a sense of wonder in their manifold interactions with the worldly and mundane. They have the power to weave ordinary knowledge into mystery, and they extend the promise to renew one's childlike wonder.

The poems comprising the "angels" portion of this work fall into the loose categories of natural, human, supernatural, and social events. Angels become embodied in material settings—in the currents of everyday life—and I seek to capture their humor, their reverence, and their playfulness therein. The "visitors" portion portrays angels as human messengers, as manifestations of the divine, as harbingers of good news. These come from a series I wrote while living at Mepkin Abbey, a Trappist community in South Carolina.

This introduction would not be complete without invoking Rainer Maria Rilke: "If the Angel deigns to appear, it will be because you have convinced him, not by tears but by your humble resolve to be always beginning — to be a Beginner!" ("Letters to Merline," 1919–1922).

Angels and Visitors is my humble beginning.

ANGELS OF KEYHOLES

The angels of keyholes have grown thinner and thinner
tightening through the brackets only an eye can pass
curved negative space, hips and torsos in aperture,
turn of a key's own slant, an idiosyncratic sleight of hand
wedge of light, an angel gives a reply in a familiar click.
They have become thin as a blade and dim of visions
braced in steel of a cold stainless polish.

Angels of keyholes no longer tumble in the lock of a door,
gone the patina of copper, their golden aureoles,
jambs reduced to a sliding silence.
Angels of keyholes have turned enigmatic, cryptic
digital and absent
a few numbers and letters
a magnetic strip on a card
soon we will no longer know how to hear them
let them carry us through the threshold
our souls and eyes in anticipation
a salute over the transom.

ROADSIDE ANGELS

Rhythmic lights the mirrors deflect over the sounds of music booms
dancers glide and contort their G-stringed booties and sequined breasts.
D.J. Al calls their names
tags for fantasies—Rosie, Lil, Vanity, Hilt, Angie.
They cross the proscenium out of the shadows
offer every turn of their limbs to the flames of patrons' gazes
in folds and counterfolds for their lascivious imaginations,
beer-steeped visions divest them to a last pearl ornament
reborn Eve, Venus lipped-wet out of a foaming sea.

Each reveals the flesh under the flesh.
High-heeled Gina struts the floor,
straddles a metal bar lifting her feet to the ceiling
and fully exposed, slides down
   to curl her legs around the shiny stainless rod.

Under the strobes these women are butterflies
multicolor beams flutter immaterial polka-dots over their bodies,
spangled gleams and powdered flesh.
The dawn's slit under the door will soon take them back
shred their wings
cast them to flightless lives joining the plying ant rings on the highway
in and out, suburban, and work-going.

PRECINCT ANGEL

Coffee sooner or later chars —leaving the rim of the hot plate
encrusted with dregs at the bottom of the pot where the scouring sponge
can't reach, and Sergeant McEntry will curse the night clerk at the cusp of
    dusk.
Black, indelible crown, angels of Hell should wear.
The door opens, closes, everyone measured by the ruler over the frame,
a moving eye glass on the ceiling reminds you who enters here
is to be seen, deposited, typed and profiled,
    print marked, digitized to a bare face
perhaps heard, if insistent to his own demise—short or long sojourner,
a same shuffling under the desk.
Precinct Angel of many cousins—Lost-and-Founds, confessor's box,
    insomniacs'
tell-tale hearts, and see-through mirror's detectives, and police blotters.
Angel of the perennial unlucky shoplifter, the stumbling youngster
a smell of ether on his breath
and after midnight will puke
a smell of perfume on his breath.
No sun, no sleep, flickering neon pulsing like a tortured eyelid,
    rasp voices on a radio
patrols in and patrols out, a hand touching a holster.
The precinct Angel takes a break at the end of a crowded bench, in the
    hold
he tries to recollect with deep frown wrinkles over his brows, a name, a
    number
the last in the instant before the blue lights and tightening iron-grip of the
    cuffs
gate opening and closing till morning and whoever stands up loses his
    seat—
a ubiquitous why are you in to rehearse a move in the antechamber an
    insider's story.

EXTERMINATING ANGEL

After Annie Leibovitz's Sarajevo

Imprints of fanned feathers in the wake of disappearing
the wind powdering snow embossing against the ground
the emerging flight motions in between the repose of her head and torso,
a blond auburn abandonment of a woman supine in a heap of leaves

and long after a lazy breakfast put away
a dent in a pillow, plissé of a bed sheet
or maybe distant ripples from a swimmer
eyes to the sky, lily buds of her breasts
the water self-erasing imprints of her motions.
Angels pass by in an elevated silence
inexplicable fragrance of an almost palpable light stream.

A war correspondent in Kosovo displays the shot of a bike flat against the
    tarmac
front wheel spinning a red arc above the fender
a comet of splattered blood exploding its head over the handlebar,
abstract expressionist hand whose blind artist is a triggered rocket
mortal orb from an exterminating Angel crushing its wings.

QUARTZ ANGEL

A translucent body, crystalline shales
the quartz, a brittling stone of multiple-edge pyramids
angels borrow layered angles for their chevroned wings.
Quartz regulates hectic currents
its atomic valence equal to sand and storm solarized to lapis lazuli
time fluidity dripping regularly to the beats of a watch.
Angels of quartz, hertzian companions of lunar winds
gloss of silica as born of sands to sands they return
grains of drowsiness left in the corners of your dreamy eyes
Angels of quartz are no gems—no glamour of diamonds
discreet and stoic—shadowing pacemakers
erratic secrets into the human heart.

ANGEL OF METAL

not heavy
light metal
scraps and aluminum cans,
Angel of crashed cars gutted in junkyards
floating under sulfuric lights
after the press has silenced bodies to thin corrugated sheets.
Punched roofs collect stars into mosquito pools.

Angel of five continents
over a lost brotherhood of assembly-line workers
and salesmen who slap a fast deal on the customer's back,
angel that returns late sitting at a kitchen table
counting and recounting to the last installment.

Angel in disguise of Julio Gonzalez's *"Femme se coiffant"*—
her double-self shadows on the white wall of the museum,
celestial movements completing her toilette
gaunt, lean montage of rods and iron plates casting her image
slanted and ungraspable ghost through the mirror metal.

ANGEL OF DUST

Alpha and Omega of our world
insidious guest present in every room
dancing in a late sun beam through a dormer
in time marbling every object with the prints of invisible fingers,
the angel of dust passes by,
Achoo in a breath,
sonorous and dismissed,
erased at the sweep of a feather
tail floating high in the sky to the smallest atoms of our bones
sister of helium and hydrogen
secret agent of a cosmic big bang
Angel of dust, our sibling,
stuff of the earth
we are made from
return to.

ANGEL OF CLAY

For Jane

Earth to earth ware
   wet, lean, or fat, water sleek
      smoothing sooth, clean out of deep dug dirt
for the vessel, wheel turned
   contoured and shaped out of hands
      palms supple, conjoining and parting
potter's Angel—praying and making
   the hollowed out calls light inside the vessel dark
      belly of a pot full of an incessant echo of the sea
color tells the clay malleability
   two handles ear-shaped, down to the bottom
      stretch of its neck to receive, fill in, pour out
raised and praised to a jar
   same clay from Siloam poulticed for the blind to see
the potter fired kiln and its Angel, solid and disappearing
quick presence, evanescent in the air like a genie.

THE MAGNETIC ANGEL

gathers and scatters by the force an invisible hand
all things metal—a knife and a spoon in a drawer
a disused alarm clock has drawn hip to spine.
Chef-knife holder its black strip plays to a fast hand
clinging in a snap to a counter gravity vibrant at every blade,
small glittering figures—Nefertiti, Curious George,
Captain Nemo, Miss Green Bayou frog, digits and world currencies,
Mary's crowned head, all holding forget-me-not notes, promises,
    yesterday's gones,
a grocery list never taken to the store
they keep the white bareness of the fridge filled and changing like a
    billboard
the magnetic Angel all forgiven
what it hangs, sticks, and dismisses,
the gliding letter puzzle waiting for a change of order
the cover of the night will bring a new meaning
a palindrome of your desire read back and forth
reconstitutes tastes from recipes giving to other tongues
the magnetic Angel conjures its invisibility calling appetites without words
as nights and days always active
stars, moon, waters' motions, a guest of the tides
pulsing lodestones the angel repeats and sets back,
converging and diverging of a same embrace, silent and magic, enigmatic.

CELLULAR ANGEL

It is the Angel of here and there,
of voices—canned, digitized, algorithmic,
then reopened in another place like an accordion
vowels spilled out into another ear decompressed from its bellow.
The space of dichotomy passed along cell towers
parsing small star echoes of satellites
the brain transmits neurologic from cochlea to fired-up synapses,
the street itself a tympanum of a dislocated conversation.
A voice, assertive, walking up
ground line—as it used to be—tethered by poles
in the cradling of distances that traveled
analog, lip-lisped through a receiver, copper wires.
Angel of an absence in figments of voices
as today, the couple, uncoupled, in a personal concertation
I follow for a while the other half in absentia with her better half
exposed in a schism
mundane details of a trip, dress to buy for a cousin
present reconstituted—a dialogue of two places
conjoined—Angel's wings stretched, then vibrant
into missing and missed—from a passing window
someone playing
Dexter's What is this thing called Love
in my pocket—self-dialed, a voice talks
pink spilled Myrtle, blooms crushed under my shoes
how could we be of two places—displaced
asymmetrical—call and response
Deus Canticum—Angel of here and there—in one body.

ANGEL OF RAIN

Under his breath the Angel of Rain extends his dominion,
eternity resounding under a tin roof,
whimsical to the winds, too much or too sparse,
heretic Angel to the calls of prayers,
his incipient moment contradicting the weatherman.

One piece to the present
the Angel of Rain repeats himself into rosaries of drops,
ripples the mist of a refreshing caress
faces waiting at the pedestrian crossing.
He drinks dust from deepening arroyos
lights a desert to an ephemeral flash of emerald
draws curtains over sail boats across the horizon.

Angel of Rain who replenishes thirst
losing himself in streams to a neverending, never-ending return,
Angel of Rain appears and disappears the length of his supple body
    through a gargoyle
whispers waiting to be revealed inside an umbrella
his present gleaming through the spray of an awning over a deserted
    avenue.

MOSQUITO ANGELS

Except for the driest places, nowhere they cannot be found,
bodies appearing and disappearing through the air
Angels of shadows, gracile legs, springs of a jumper hardly visible
they populate the smallest places of moisture,
crease of a leaf, old tires that rim water inside, saucers, shallows and pools.
They come to your ears, leave a swelt on your cheek bone.
fly in counter light of dusk
conniving attackers in sortie.
Call for a blood meal truly guides them.
Wind born tigers, striped torsos and legs
they evade any movement of air to slap them,
taste the dew sweetness and replenish the surface of a pond with their
    eggs.
Chemical warfare will only displace them -
vampire angels with suction needle mouths,
intentive pursuers they don't care what they carry, yellow fever, Ebola,
    dengue
a new strand of flu, classic malaria, just the benign rash of their lancing.
Nimble and gone in the air, they question the goodness of creation,
agents of theodicity, snout proboscis, the culprit agent
the female, usual suspect in her seeking proteins to spawn
while the male placid and pacifist feeding on nectar, harmless,
winged angels of stings the cold will trap their larva in ice
awaiting perniciously the next thaw for their feasting.

ANGEL OF FROST

The frost holds a stillness under the cloche of a sky
around the blocks people have covered plants
stretched tents like angels protecting the feeblest ones
each street lines a corridor of frigid milkweed lights.
By the front door of your house two kumquat trees
their orange lanterns the cold brightens and sweetens under their skins
the insidious frost passes inside your sleeves,
expends your lungs to a prickly veil inside.
The frost asks for the present to be lived in, loved, and endured.
Tomorrow yards will be hecatombs of flimsy limbs.
It is not the provision you believe you made, salvation of roots.
On the way home, the bundle of a man on a stoop
his face covered inside a cap—
you left by his side a bill and a bar of chocolate warm from your pocket.
Strange and close to bend and hear the breath of a man—
air from a far place
inside/ outside
life and frost.

ANGEL OF WINDS

A day of gray smoothing all angle
colors backlit at the thinnest piercing ray
the emerald lawn each blade standing, leaves tossing and rolling.
Head against the wind, gust lashing sands at my eyes and skin,
I get off my bike pushed off like a sail,
my gloves on the bench, empty-handed, scud slightly to wave back
a short hello off the yellow leather fingers
and edged fall to the ground.
The angel of winds pushes them further to run after
wind's joke to show the strength of the invisible
catch'me and follow'me to no end and purpose but its own
"you hear its sound, but cannot tell where it comes from
or where it is going." (John 3.8)

ANGELS OF TREES

They found themselves deep in the kernel flesh, their own rings of Saturn,
demi-wings the loam opens in the darkness, dormant mosses seeping
    dreams
constitutive of rules—genetic—an acorn of oak's lineage
years in seasons, seasons in years
elevating the sky to their leaves
to take cover in the great cuneiforms of their twigs.
What nourishes? Above and below
as much of rains, stars, moons, heliotropes
as to clay, rocks, water seeking roots extending their dominions.
Firs like green bonnets on the snow-covered slopes,
climbing plumes, coiffes of Royal palms circumscribing an oasis,
the inverted Japanese magnolia budding its mauve votive on bare
    branches.
Trees that breathe their meditations to the world—cool and rejuvenating,
what do they say to birds? Tribal emperors of their species
polyglots of sedentary lives,
deep eyes that never die in the inner rims marking their years.
Trees felled their own coffins floating down rivers to the forgetfulness of
    the sea,
fuel, furniture, last angel of trees to the luck of knocking wood.

ANGELS OF SEA

Angels are not accountants,
subtracters, abstracters,
aggregators, contenders, in time and space,
no linearity—hear the angels pronounce the inarticulate life of your soul.
On the beach, Angels of sea partake of infinite lines, sand and sky,
always in motions, never losing, gaining in distance
here—far and close—every atom of spume
iodine, kelp, they give to breathe
further than the sea can map out the world
Angels of sundry names in one geography
joyful of the spray they refresh, rebirth on your face
your steps they have erased bringing back from your coming ashore
in bodies and minds they who no body, no substance—all essence of the
    sea
Angels that endure all weathers
never sink, conquer all abyss, touch the floor of world,
surreal over falling snows on the ocean.

ASTHMATIC ANGEL

You are caught in the noose of your neck
and let go to a free fall through a trap door—
the snap of your nape
every knuckle of your spine runs out like falling dominoes ,
fish mouth of empty scream wriggling on the bank of a stream
incomprehensible pain running dry to the bulging of your eyes
as if delivered from a long anger bursting a malevolent tumor of revenge.

A knot inside your throat
the tightening you fear will choke you to a last flight,
a breath of atmosphere before all what you can proffer
a silent cry, haruspication of your own lungs.
You suddenly slack the tensed muscles of your agony

a white drip fluid invading the deep provinces of your sleep
asthmatic angel of your cataleptic state.

Your little self-game of dying   you, my sweet hysteric
your faint fainting leaving you the abandoned inhabitant of your body
disrobed, pale angel, half-naked on a cold linoleum.

ANGEL OF FALLING LEAVES

Of eyes, he possesses the deciduous foliage of his dispossession
clear view of autumn disrobing every bough
wind swirls plummeting plane tree leaves
widening sky to the maple palmate waving red hands,
the simple twirls of the oak the mat echo of an acorn follows.
Angel of leaves kids kick in the air shuffling sycamores shedding covers
he gives a chill to the spine of exposed trees,
the torve catalpa October erases its last blooms for mysterious falling
    pods.
He has strewn golden wing leaves through the woods
taking the sun to a last splendor in decline,
the eminent cold passing a brief breath over our necks.
Season of burrs and drying seeds to the ground
limbs hard and exposed to the strength of their roots
a dying for a return, Christ-like, left harvest expectations the wind
    gleaned,
Demeter's specter in the forthcoming shadows of winter.

DEPARTING ANGEL

For Elsbeth

Falling from a magnolia
leaves sway an angel's way
bristle over the path of an old woman
slow, crushing the crumbling litterfall
her feet and cane to the gristle of her bones.
She pushes her lanky toes to her last home
her breath deepening, floating in the pellucid atmosphere
the cold air where she and her Angel companion
side by side each small crackle closer and closer to a final destination
the fog enveloping beyond, above, below,
inside her eyes, into her hair
where suspended luminous in the autumn she stays
double of her angel gone off her guard.

HOLY ANGEL, LAST AUCTION

The line lengthened, longer than the rope circling the courtyard
twisting at turns, front gate to side chapel door
a procession of prattlers, speculators of troves
nuns' testaments, memories to souvenirs, holy trinkets
armoires, chiffoniers, robes, evening dresses to crumpled habits,
old day top-stove irons, a few dark-wood valets. frocks.
Holy Angel put to visitors, bargain finders, gawkers, nostalgiacs,
till all goes in the cadence of subtractions, purchases,
pros and amateurs, we too stood in the midst of small talks.
A plump woman stenciled a name on a brick
she folded back into her planner on today's page
as if memory lived embossed in lines and filigrees,
tangible like colored glasses and furnishings,
the nuns' dining tables and rattan chairs, double-sided confession boxes
unwanted pews, a disused gueridon, scrapbooks
pictures losing gloss, faltering into remote stories
"I was there, playing, prancing from stairs to stairs, a woman in lines
speaks loud recollections eight, mimicking angels' flights."

WINTER ANGELS

Angels lose their halos,
the small ones of a lower order, plastic and hollow
unscrewed and garaged, they smell the winter hay
black robes of contractor bags.
They sleep long starry nights
    barely disturbed by the coming of the snow plough man.

The larger plaster ones, tarped with a first layer of soft bed foam,
yellow color of their first dawn,
a blanket on top where they snug their wings
kept tugged and roped under a canvas.
Snow will pile and winds carve a blue hue refulgence of crystalline
    shadows.

The marble and alabaster ones, all weather, stilled in their élan,
high on their toes, wing-stretched.
snow, flakes after flakes, sticks and double-draws them,
snow over snow,
angelic whiteness lost over the field overwritten by snowmobile tracks.

When Spring will come they will catch a warmer breath of Easter,
a gift divine passing over humans,
coming back of birds
their glyphs over ground and the piercing of flowering bulbs.
Divested Winter Angels return to the light of the sky, shedding to a new
    life,
open to the valley, companionable of thoughts and prayers.

SNOW ANGEL

You made a snow angel
I dusted off your back, the white powder
more than shades of your wings you left on the white flaked grass
like dragonfly's frenzy wings batting over ground
hands can't catch and eyes hold still
in the blueness of yours—ice crystal cerulean in high atmosphere
word images sharp and vanishing on my tongue like a strong alcohol.
I saw a flight of fights inside your irises
and a reflecting milky sky crossing your eyes
love and madness for the lack of loving love
snow fleas under the firs' branches frisk at their jumping,
aspens turning bronze, long heart shapes harrowing
and a dead still snow angel,
frozen imprints that turned a slow sundown carrousel.

ANGEL'S LINE

If the Angel deigns to appear, it will be because you have convinced him, not by tears but by your humble resolve to be always beginning—to be a Beginner.

RAINER RILKE. *LETTER TO MERLINE*

Whiteness on the page
     space between spaces
splicing words
     salt and spices
voices and vowels. Angels
come and go.
Wing scratch
pencil tip quick
letters shaped off hand
tail cloud dissipates
words on a somnambulist's lips:
back to the line
a face appears
eyes on snow blinking back at the sky
the illumination in a coal mine the lunge of a pike sparks
burst of a face in mind and mine explosion

not mine, not yours,
     Angels'

blowing in the margins
brief and a bit clumsy with their adolescent wings
     Byzantine with their meticulous gold orbs and delicate attachments.
Go with the Angels a voice says
     Con los Angeles the Cuban guide points at the road
meaning this way down hill will ease your body weightlessly
     towards a wide-embracing sea
          waves fleeting beyond the Malecon
               wind pushes, erases

between sea and sky
     God's first words ever about to open the
       thinnest white line.

REFUGEE ANGEL

Angel where do you come from
unshaven, hair matted with the restlessness of sleep
a woman bedraggled, children in train, shawls
colors from times of feast and peace,
   scarves wrapped around their necks up to their ears
and every place you try to enter, a door,
no home behind.

You chew the grind of the road, breathed the desert sand of hunger.
Borders no longer dots on a map,
assortments of incertitude,
waiting lines, X-ray glass room, ports of entry in between ferries and
    death,
blind yells for passports, affidavits, sniggering agents of body searches

life bottlenecked to a single eyehole of a sentry box.
Still, children play in the narrowing lanes of tent camps,
the elders skip the daily meal, weight of famine for a chance to break away
hostages of two warring sides, the camp squeezes in diseased dreams and
    dystopia.

The mouth of a river should be a place of freeing waters
ostia, a rejuvenation against death—
against the banks, canisters grappled out a lethal cornucopia
a cluster bomb spilled over roads and playgrounds,
Aleppo, no pepper spice, a city nerve-shocked in bombs and gas.

The angel knows the measure of human bitterest vindications, fire of
    revenge
the erring path, a weary mother may take triggering lightening into noon,
feet follow feet from seas through snows, rivers, tarmacs—steps erasing
    steps.
In Mölndal, Sweden, news reports from over banked-up street sludge

Ms. Mezher—a social worker in the asylum stabbed in the line of
    peacemaking duty
"en ängel som vill göra gott" the local paper says:
    "an angel who wants to do good".

ANGELS OF RAFTERS

pass through floor boards and ceilings
at the crack of dawn and death of dusk

briefly enter the space of our lives
from the attic or under the house.

They know the place
history, its hearsays

the former tenant, an opera seamstress
pinning paddings, shoulders and breasts

absent actors and actresses she plays in the mirror
quickly redoing her lipstick for her lover coming at the door.

Angels of rafters recollect everyone by the weight of their steps
the timber of their voices filtering through the beams

a passing shadow across a dormer
a faint talc smell when you stretch over the floor

they are witnesses to the deep breathing of a daughter in prayer
a muttering voice reading the lost and found between the lines of a
    newspaper

Angels of rafters who seldom ever offer any encounter.

ANGEL OF IGNORANCE

Every morning mist arises from the margin of the windowpane.
It is not unusual to hear the revving of an engine by the 3:30 am on the
   blue digital clock,
no sound of steps, no noise of departure,
a space opens to silence between doors shutting.
Along the dewy bayou road,
Damsel flies mimic red leaf stems, filigree translucid leaves of their thin
   wings
cerulean as tungsten, naiads unmolten in their apparitions

light equilibrium of match sticks—
lives of seeking and hiding, glass walls of our still sleepy paths
the lizard—*pequeño lartigo*, on column ledge

furtive emerald pulsing over an acanthus leaf
How the neighbor boy with his speech impediment slowly extracts
each vowel from the deep well of his lung and brain,
aphasia of reordering the fault line of a phrase
hesitating, stumbling, letting go—your wheel has flattened your bike

you will walk home empty shoe,
as God speaks among us in the folds to the clearing of our deepest desires
what the Angel knew we didn't know in the side steps of our noon
   shadows
because of him kings shall stand speechless,
for those who have not been told shall see,
those who have not heard shall ponder it. (Is: 52: 13)

NEIGHBOR ANGELS

For Angels rent the House next ours,
Wherever we remove—'

Emily Dickinson

Shall the poet's hand be guided by meaning, sounds
or both, in a figure, dark or light, an Angel muse
in what words create as small planets
recomposing visions in their atoms from lips to ears through atmosphere.
News of the world in roots and leaves
water and air—winds and oceans, fluid sounds and chants,
thirst at the end of a faucet,
News speaks in voices from other women and men,
and at night the radio waves transmit endlessly
the boxed voices of our heads—creatures
nocturnal—foxes, owls, train conductors, nightwatchmen
jars and certain types of felines, satyrs and maidens
the nova pulses casting its inspirational rays
erased into the day it influences,
all what is life and death
the shanties of our dreams, the diurnal, clear and real,
or the reverse? For where Angels dwell,
apparitional and palpable, our neighbors
"the house next ours
wherever we remove—"

CEMETERY ANGEL

From above the cemetery the Angel stands to the sky
feminine into the blue a single cloud magnifies
wings on its back, head sightly bowed
the sun rays underlying its alabaster body
like a swimmer tenses and concentrates before a somersault high above
an immensity it already reaches from the stone
a domain outside the gravity the city no longer pertains,
and blinking to the sun am I left between the living and the dead?
At the edge Esplanade Cemetery across from Cabrini High School
the rambling of a bus, bicycle bells, car exhausts
in a sault of salvation, the Angel let us return to the busy, weighty streets.
A lean, tall cypress like a sole black incandescent flame
the Angel's silhouette opens the space
we having peered through the ogive of the sky
trudge the weight of our human way.

ANGEL OF ROPES

Whizz of the air, twisted
strands over strands
knot of a naught
eye of a lasso,
angel of ropes
sailor's deep friend
sweat and salt
through his hands to the bitter end,
angel of ropes that twists
double hitch knots
rappel to rappel
it climbs above the rocks
sneak to a mountain peak,
angel of ropes that multiplies forces of pulleys
and passes bricks high
over the ledge of a building,
angel of bolas
with the chime of its weights
sibilant in the air
stops short a running guanaco,
angel of tug of war
tensed of a taut string about to snap,
angel of ropes that grieves
noose eye the executioner
placed around a neck,
a naked tie of a last breath
through a trap
that echoes a tolling bell
pulled up and down,
a rope to the length of a belfry,
angel of ropes that dangles
tight to a chimney
down to a blind alley
and dusts its wings off

silver grey from ashes,
angel of ropes
that can bind, secure, and free
a cargo against the strength of the ocean.

THE ANGEL OF WALLS

stands at the top
the call of his breath,
susurrus of the wind begging to jump over,
the newfound land of an unweeded flower garden.

He sits at the edge looking right and left, up and down
seeps a beer, gives a sigh, a free breath between public and private,
his spine dented with broken bottles, glint from a razor wire.

The angel of walls takes the sun to its last red crimson on the bricks
cool to inescapable stars with a blind eye for a graffiti artist.
The angel of walls lends an ear to a knock of welcome
I hear you" in reply through the hollow divide of the concrete
a tapped alphabet, discrete, almost intimate, to the inmate's knuckles.

The Angel of walls knows all inside-out
a double face Janus that never sees eye to eye.
Sometimes a ray, a grace, insight framed through a window—
a back and a front,
face against the wall for a silenced schoolboy
back against the wall to the deafening dead boom of a firing squad.

This angel knows the two sides of partitions,
what separates and what unites—East and West, line of confrontation
Wailing's, Hadrian's, China's never ending,
Berlin's, DMZ's, Tortilla's, Chernobyl's,
betrayal of its soundings in echoes of hopes and prayers.
The angel's legs dangle, he jumps and never falls
strides of acrobat, aerialist's grand vista,
the angel takes a mile of freedom every inch of his heels.

GARBAGE ANGELS

Hunched back garbage truck
the munching jaws of its drum compacting trash
clinks and clanks, bell ring, come and go,
swirl its belly swallows
yellow eyes in the coming morning
black head of a snake
slithering through every street
tossed lids and bins in its wake
sprite garbage men in pairs fanning in and out
tight and left to the dribbling of garbage drips
in cadences of their expert grips
decomposing a movement in slow motion
an unobserved ballet
a short, a long, in-step, out-step
lobbing of a plastic bag
a pursuit from door to door
the rank belly of the city
yesterday's parties
cook's old bits
end life of toasters and muted radios—
terminal place, dumpster, archeology of memories
the metropolis 'great landfill
cemetery of maimed and lame objects,
indigestible trophies from passing heroes.
Before joggers, night clerks, hotel workers hit the Quarter
garbage angels sway out of the city the latest pick of the day.

ANGEL OF SMALL CHANGE

Paper changed to jingles
bill breaker—paid and unpaid
the angel of small change
spread of scattered coins over the ground
flip of a chance narrowed to yes and no
heft of their gathering in the obscurity of a purse
the metal they bear not worth the value of their names
mint of their heads and tails fingered to weariness and grim
proverbial last penny of a debt
angel of small change that comes to the rescue, spare and wingless,
to foot the bill on tip toe, square a tip on top of a tab.

LOAN ANGEL

You called anonymously, merely revealing your first name. No face I know to put on. You said in a white voice payments were late. You restated it plainly. Could I have felt an innuendo of reproach? You were not asking how it could be—had I no money? How had I spent the inheritance from an aunt on a baby grand piano, not even tried to return a dime on what I had borrowed? Even with my arpeggio, music from the twelve most celebrated arias, it won't fly. I was just delaying, and later I will have to pay even more, penalties and late fees. Humbly, I would have said, I know. You also stated I had to give my current address and phone numbers with no incognito. Maybe your name was Ricardo, Victor—something I may recall. You will call again almost anonymously, but I won't let you go. I'll put a face over your voice, unmask you till my loans outgrow your own children's retirements. Will I make dues and progress on my instalments? You will be the one that will have to inquire, and find out about my health wanting to know if I am about to blow the balloon over my dividends. So, you too will grow old, older that is like anyone but your ghost. Will I let it go or put a face on you like a spell? What was your name . . . Antonio . . . Victor . . . Angelo, something like that—another name perhaps, familiar and a bit foreign, and yet sounding always the same?

KITCHEN ANGEL

The kitchen Angel dances at the tip of the long hand
between each tick of the clock
pliés and pirouettes, a little ballet,
her body concentrates and dissipates
in subtle whiffs, archangelic clouds out of a roasting pan,
a little bubbling chant inside the oven—
a kitchen angel, bright white wings from the back
her forearms turned copper by the stove heat
a blue reflection from the salamander
where she pulls quick a gratin out before it burns
kitchen angel of flour dusted shoulders
her celestial breath over the dough
she mists the hearth in a vaporized halo
kitchen angel passing through the back door to the dumpster
water and dish liquid foaming in the sink
she sings an old Cuban sailor's song
bursting to shouts and stampedes *la chinga! Se vienne la migra*!
kitchen angel with Vietnamese hands,
her stout African feet that can dance to the clinging of dishes,
kitchen angel wrestling at every turn of the hour
the pegs wavering waiters' slips ready to fire
kitchen angel that never surrenders
slumbering in the pantry,
blurry eye by a crate of lemons,
scullery lending a magic touch to every dish
angel climbing to no heaven
a hovel in the attic.

ROOFER ANGELS

Left on the edge of the tin gutter
the metal glitters with frost
linear skyscraper ladder to the blue, voiceless and clear azure.
The Hondurans roofers gone with the blaring music
rhythm for burly men threading thin on the slats
black shingles replaced, new
rain unpocked writing slate of the sky,
pails clank, garrulous songs and country bandoneons, *chistes* and curses
a scintillant frost, nail heads shine like stars
Angels gone of Jacob's ladder white frozen and snow flaked
teaming up with blows nail guns, boots and hooks they made it
evanescent illegals, redeployed to other places to cover the storm rage,
houses and yards they looked from atop, transients, landscape in their
    eyes
stretching all the way to the wall, sands and arroyos
saguaro, and barbed wires of the frontera.

ANGEL HORSE

Stirrups, legs supple against the flanks,
his horse jumps, syrup of sweat under the saddle
hoofs suspended in the air.
Flying started there Pegasus tells
and the equine intelligence, unicorn,
muscle bound and tensed, a cosmic animal
rapture of its own journey—where to?

To the fairground where the way circles and circles
faster and faster
      a merry-
          go-
              round
a round each horse can almost bite the tail ahead
and what to chase—steeples,

cheers and clamors,
luck of a bettor under his hat
horses run and run pursuing each other
for the many gamblers who become debtors of their own fate
the angel horse, hoofless, passes by.
End race—flip or ship to the slaughter.

CAMBER

The alignment angel (*sic*) of a wheel on a car. The angel (*sic)* from the top of
the wheel to the bottom. If you have negative camber the top of the wheel is in
(towards the car) If you have positive the bottom of the wheel is towards the car.

FROM CAMBER, URBAN DICTIONARY.COM, POSTED JANUARY 21, 2004

How many angles to shimmy on the tip of a pin?
The alignment angel knows better—the slant of the camber
from up and down, down and up that can go far as the curve of the earth.
The wheel that turns and turns
a sun of its own appearing and disappearing further than the day,
the swish of its spin like a kiss to the road in the rain,
negative or positive, giving in or giving out,
like the wear of a shoe—introvert or extrovert.
The driver arrives home to find his pregnant wife resting on the sofa
the small her back,
his hand soft on the camber of her spine
her belly round of expectations, taut, perfect like a wheel
of a wheel within, a hub of life inside
a small planet in a galaxy of placenta, cosmogony of cells
cogs and cogs in turns of chromosomes
what life aligns, in coming and going only the wheel angel knows,
the belly button of the newborn with the lunar twist of an equinox.

ANGELS OF LOST THINGS

A casual angel of two wings—one side bright white
the other a shade of blue grey—space and time
   meeting to the median of its body
between the missing of what is lost to memory.
A hat on a bench, trains pass by
the owner far and gone suddenly adjusting his hair
the missing of his mean brim suddenly palpable under his hand.
An intended last letter, sealed with a breath of regret
stamped, unaddressed, between pages of "Home on the Road—Dinner,
   Drinks and Amenities."
Hand fumbling blind in a pocket, an act manqué
a key, a wedding band left on the side of a sink.
Angel of lost things in the shadows of a hurried clerk
free from the burden of her bag—book, table, lipstick, and apple of
   impatient hunger.
Angel of retraced steps in hopes of the imagined blue glove to materialize
apparitional as the negative space between leaves and fingers over ground.
Angel of lost things evanescent as a comb dropped in a pond
all things return to the common of a black hole,
memory of what is missing to the oblivion of a tomb.

ANGELS OF THREADS AND BUTTONS

Through the thread of a contrail
a plane holds in the sky
a pinpoint two dimensional against the blue
and melts into the infinite
a wafer after taste lasting a bit longer in the clear winter solstice.

Thread Seraph of his brother, Angel of Buttons
closing the key-hole line of a jacket,
little lunules of ivory, plastic, wood, bone, or bamboo
holding tight to the twist of a thumb and index
closing in, opening out to the mood of a season.

Loose and weary buttons hang dangerously by a last thread
the cold of their absence
empty handed
drop and roll,
drop and roll
to oblivion
or caught,
in a small tin box,
till mended, eyes full of a thread needled
up and down, up and down
twisted and knotted
a deft hand renewed to the clasping fingers of an old habit.

ANGEL OF WOODS

He knocks on trunks
the faraway sound of a clock
hectic woodpeckers stubborn stutterer
the forest knows his deep radiance
his wings stretched under the clearing.
In season, chestnuts scatter prickly urchins
shiny brown eyes' insights.
Angel of Woods the lost travelers follow
tracking the mossy sides of trees
and a legend grows in whispers from the mountains
the long rustle of dusk across the crowns
orange moon lit anamita, *Fly Agaric,*
root stubs, long scar vulvas of wind-felled branches
white phallic ink mushrooms, witches' puff balls,
and much further in the night a syncopating light
where a silenced, old wood mill stands.
How soon trembling trucks beyond the disused tracks quiver running
    halos,
we self-deceived by our childhood fears, ferns closing behind our foot
    path
walked long and not so far from our camp,
and kept mute on the way home,
a bit weary under our eyes from the fernery penumbra
the angel of wood, cyclopic knot, keeping vigil spread-wing on the kitchen
    table.

ANGELS OF VISIONS

Angels, brief and swift
parabola of their disappearance.
The sky traces for a second
a scintillating syntax fused over the starry parchment
intense as the razor-edged signature of a skater on untouched ice.

Angels alter an unmovable sky
a blank page calls for their coming back
illuminating presence of relucent light they left behind,
the eye's after-image suspended magically, Saint Elmo's fire,
evaporated as in a dreamy smell of ether
palm lines brief of three lives:

Arthur Rimbaud's smiling at the *Wasserfalt blond,*
juvenal greenness pungent and lasting of a new fruit
true core of wood swaying forest murmuring the boat's keelson
"Au cabaret vert,"

Hart Crane's pacing the seaport's streets
the marina chancelled whiteness over a desert blue sea
the same land that slips under the ocean
movements of sounds, chrysalides of corrals,
bones silent to anagrammatized dead letters,

Keith Douglas—gunpowder smell lingers
and whiffs off like a mortar after-blow,
Corpses buried in sands
love and anger leave behind a rued odor
dogs decipher in a stalked city,
charred tanks and sand gripped equipment
Vergissmichnitch

the sky recedes, wider turn
to Cerulean ink on night's page
encyclical, shining paths of corposant satellites

milk flower, a cloudburst on a bare stem,
an angel's hand sows in the wind.

ANGEL OF HAY

The Angel of hay has straw sun beams in his hair
a smell that quietens the field, open-wide,
all what is baled off a season stacked in the darkness
a few rays piercing through the roof guild,
dust and scratchy stubbles in peace for the moment
the weight of every straw lighter than the air can make a ton held together.

The straw misused for burning at the stake
in billows of smoke that choke before the high flames envelop the body
before she disappears with the smell of burned hair and flesh,
calcination to the bones, sainthood can't yet displace with a holy scent.

The man of straw—taken for a goat to no escape,
scarecrow of falsity under the cover of human eye,
the Angel of straw—thatched and stacked up
rain will compact, leave dry folds overhead in a barn of bats and swallows
early July night in new stars of harvest time
Angel of straw collects and recollects
hayricks built in circles standing still as about start a dance
giddy gig to a red moon, dark edges of the fields
a world turning as if all in a flame could go, illuminate
the earth half lit, half dark turning its face.

ANGEL OF ILLUSIONS

The One and only One, who passed over the human life and resurrected,
the many in bronze, ivory, gold, marble, ebony,
alabaster, onyx full of wishes and fantasies lagged out,
pulled back from the seer's mouth like a toothache into infected gum until
    rot-rooted out.
Mercury misidentified in the Constantin Basilica
the faithful prayed for a Saint Jude in the ancient powers of vatic dreams.
Had not Monica for all her son's scurrilous life conceived him a bishop?
Augustin himself got rid of a toothache by his friends' prayers at
    Cassiciacum?

Oils of prayer from the heathen temples still in currency, burning auras
    and glistening bodies
a dry mother from Amasya was bestowed milk to nurse all the village's
    children against a curse,
not so graced, Peter the Iberian still called on the oracle to save his
    daughter.
The supernatural brushed sleeves with the sorcerers in the cloth of Saint
    Remigius,
the plague assailed the anointed parading out in wintery Rheims nearly
    barren skins to the wind
and the miracles carried their way into the fantastic,
disinterred his body scented oil and myrrh.
Theodore of Sykeon—Maria a star impregnated—shining over her gravid
    womb,
the father, worth every acrobatics of his imperial camel show, gifted an ice
    crystal diadem.
In the Palace of Heaven, Archangel Michael led a coup d'état
ousting the Devil in its many mimicking figures—human and animal.

Out of idols, the festival changed,
the healing of people inhabited niches of holy men and women
the stylite Symeon cried out a paradise regained in the desert
descending from his pillar to lend a holy hand

stopped the menstrual hemorrhagic flow
   off a woman and nefarious demons sneered.
Long after Constantine had his face coined onto the Unconquered Sun,
how many holy men under their cloaks could tell the wings of illusion
   from an Angel's?

ANGEL BIRDS OF SWAMPS

Past Bonnet Carré the swamps open wide of dark peat and tupelos
we slowly skiff through one arm of the bayou to reach button eyes of water
little sinews we paddle to the hearing of the lake.

Down to the throats we slice through the vermillion bilge
the soupiness of vegetation huddling the wintering snapping turtles and
    alligators
—a few birds—Ibis with trumpet bills, Garde Soleil bitterns

camouflaging their striped plumage to the oscillations of the reeds,
the anhingas of black togas high above dropping into the oblivion of the
    swamp.
Are those the choirs of the wetlands? Cherubs and Angels—black jet

to what eternal truth you may plunge into the murky streams
to the declining east in the principalities of the estuary.
spoonbills float in a pink cloud reddening into dusk

making a last call to go home to confound into the land,
heaven? mosquito hell? sportsman's paradise?

ANGEL OF THE NIGHT

Every day, you close the cloak of your bright outer wings over the sky,
choker of stars covers the west, you hold gardens dormant under your
    chest
city lights, aura dusting the firmament with highway bands,
commuter rails and signaling airports crisscrossing destinies.
You speak to our ears the nocturnal insects, the jars and thrilling bell
    frogs,
the relentless mosquito no hand can slap to silence,
papyrus leaves oscillate their cloudy heads to your passing breath.
The horn of a tugboat echoes through the fog rising your palpable
    presence to a watcher's face.
You move slow invading the province of our dreams in respite of our
    sights,
night walkers, rebellious insomniacs,
    belles de nuit the last call burns to a red glow,
a thief following you close in the night, hours and dreams you glide over
    our eyes
till you retreat through the blinds the chevrons of your wings
luminescent, the sun briefly merges with behind the slats,
déja vu, strange and omniscient a slight perfume of your disappearance,
erased, a slight smudge from the headlines on our hands.

TECHNICOLOR ANGELS

In their eyes colors never fade
they maintain a clairvoyance
no eye surgery needed to brush off fading contrasts
no technicolor to overlayer a new palette
angels' eyes live with no concern for dioptric
sights are visions in light, in breaths and sighs
the paint always new, the lenses shine inner isinglass
and perspective never falls to the chute of the infinite suspending all abyss
    in flight
radiant and rays angels live in and out of Newton's second prism
no optic illusion all real of major glory
the One only artist and art at once
all in colors, humans try to imitate to the image of God.
Technicolor Angels rest in the sleep of the livings,
    dream a-temporal in Black and White
the snow over the TV screen blurring into REM.

STORM ANGEL

The storm Angel takes clouds under his wings
dissimulating his ascent in air streams and brine waters.
The ubiquity of its presence fanning out in the sheaf last sun rays,
its wing open-wide canopy tipping in a last patch of blue.
Had we even noticed the slight tremors of its moving shadows
rustling more nervously in the crepe myrtles against the fence door?
Storm Angel ensconced in the small cumulonimbus of our floating minds
carrying over us ominous umbrellas of worries,
the purple filament in a torch light flashing the eyes of a thief in the night.
Storm Angel in the snarled eye of pouncing winds overwhelming the
    levees
wing-dipped drenched and flat-faced from Lake View to the Ninth Ward.
No voice over the roof tops could raise nor the hovering rotors lifting up
    survivors
uncover your apparition through the slipped off riverbed
a blind, raging maelstrom splattering swirl of terror
leaving oil-thick, muddy streets of X-marked houses with wide opened
    doors.
Angel Storm awakened in an old car seat of an empty garage,
light-beams-frozen shadows that zombie through Highway 10 deserted
    lanes
he shouts his lungs out against the night to the City Old Fathers,
Do you know where your children are?

ANGEL OF NEW SIGHT

Wind bashing, beating at doors and windows
people's voices eaten off their mouths, twist gale of sounds.

Shall we know what winds scatter wide to other places?
What they mutter blind for black eyes to land on?

A man with lost sight—Tobit—warm pigeons' droppings falling over his
   eyes
cataracts condemning him to Tenebrae.

Exile within exile his near-name-sake-son his guide
sent to retrieve a far treasure as too to meet his fate with a new turn

an Angel's way—of flesh and bones—who fished him
poultices of sturgeon livers and a dark incense to fume the jealous
   wedding monster Asmodeus

the bride a widow made live again
   from her seven husbands before the matrimonial bed
the guise of an angel to find his way

sand shaken off his sandals shedding a last scruple of doubt.

SPRING WASHED OFF ANGEL

[He] causes rain to fall on the just and the unjust.

MATTHEW 5:45

To walk in the rain as to step outside of yourself
morning gray gave way to a blue wedge, a ray and then silvered entirely
the sky within reach, let believe all will clear
dust to the ground, lanky magnolias, wet heat of cars,
and accept to be trickled, the rain beads still slower than your steps
grazes your face, your hair pulled under your hood,
your feet, each discreet, touch ground, like a monk across a cloister
and cleft of the darkening clouds,
    lightening against the adumbration of the path.
Tick, tock, tick tock that soon outpace you—
wash of heaven with no place to run in or out,
rivers of leaves, gurgling of gargoyles and gutters, your face glistens
the storm discalcing you, stripping you to a dancing shadow of yourself
against what you had set for with a bit of rebellious acedia
to ease your knees from ankyloses, grace given of this world in passing
soaked, blessed, and near shivering of Spring
just and unjust, which you are as all rained on
your eyes prickling blind, sweet lips and acidity of down pour.
You fumble the knob, drenched out naked,
strip puddles over the floor, redeemed, saved and safe, and spared from
    nothing
the whole sky, dog smell, pollens and petals, street grit, gutter silt,
the angel rain that carried you over the threshold shakes you off its wings,
    free.

ANGELS' TRUMPETS

A cascade of pale yellow blooms
upside down trumpets
angels blow to the end of their breaths,
pendulous stamens,
vases with pink lips.

If put in a bedroom, the Datura's perfume diffuses dreams
an ocean deep of sleep carrying you out of your body
amber figures of a Kamasutra bestiary,

a thieve may empty the house in front of the dreamer's unblinking eyes,
a stallion, black, like a pegasus galloping silently in the snow of the ceiling
sostienete, ciego en la montura del cielo jienete del sueño.

Seduction, avalanche of petals to a pastel lemony smell,
insidious scent reverberating in your brain
an Angel of your lover's eyes into yours,
weightless horizon flying off your lashes.

SUGAR CANE ANGEL

Cut down to the stalks, machetes long ago
harvester now, fronds fallen, stripped of leaves
to be what am called sugar cane
put through the press, juiced out
bagasse dead down to the fibers of my body,
heap of ashes, a mount of black slags to the sky
all molasses from my pith they crystalize me
amber dark, distilled, vatted, aged
rhummed me for what some lose their limbs and reasons
from my sweet good nature living in animosity with the diabetic
turned to no color, Angel white, purer and purer through the age,
turned to xxx confectionary powder
made solid into cubes, dominos, dice rolled
no winning numbers, knuckle bones of the dead
intensified sweetness of all myself, hard white dissolved in black coffee
cane king—pristine white—cane like the one signaling the blind
good and bad, Angel of magic and misery
transubstantiation of the spirit through my body
the green fairy of absinth—to the soul of Verlaine
delirium and words, sublime of poetry—sweet in the bitter and bitter in
the sweet.

JAIL ANGEL

His warm breath insinuates through bars a bit of free sky
an iron gate unlatches and latches back in an unoiled yawn
wardens confiscated his belt, the small pen knife from his breast pocket,
his very wings mistaken for a drunk's Mardi Gras gaudy contraptions,
a keno ticket, an expired passport, an over-traveled wallet
with a Saint Christopher silver medal.
All registered and sealed in a numbered bag among others,
in lines of hang up lives like cloths dumb waiting at a dry cleaner.

He takes an empty seat on a concrete bench
neon lights flicker obsessively
soon there will be no way to surmise night from day.
His shoes tap on the floor a far rhythm from a time outside.
Sunday on Franklin Square with a half brass band section
rehearsing a funeral march on the lawn,
his hands joined in slow movements—a bridge of light, a tunnel of fingers
a short prayer, clasped wings, a dark mouth with pink lips
his thumbs open and close speaking to his inner silence
white caps of hours in darker seas of regrets,
Dawn will come beyond the walls
orange like the color of jail suits and bust over the horizon the fullness of
    the sun.
He moves his head to loosen his neck, eyes blind to the ceiling
far steps, the flush of a toilet, someone let in or out
he follows the steps as a tale in his mind
ignoring the rustle of roaches circling over the floor.

ANGEL OF INSPIRATION

Always the seemingly random encounter of a precise meeting
a brief visitor and a long roadside between ditch and field.
Divides of the canes in few weeks to be cleared to a new horizon
the echoes of the birds will change
coming of cars, the stalks barrier sounds and sight.
Someone cut out a path through the canes opening to a maze deep in the
    field,
no minotaur, not many visions
    the light high from above with changing skies
no walls to climb to spy the exit.
The maze itself the shape of a skeleton key
no lock to fit in but the one of your soul,
wind blows through syllables,
linnets, sparrows nestled deep in emerald spade-shaped leaves
you walk the rough ground, smell of clay and heat
breathing a presence behind you, aspiration, inspiration
take humor—the angel of inspiration exhales
after all the angel of inspiration will only give you a start
later midway through your oeuvre she will erase, ease ear, be your
    breathing,
as it is you who found it, guided by the hand in insipience and sapience
a plagiarism of your own work,
always in progress, God given, blink of an eye, harvest to come.
The angel of inspiration already gone,
apparitional, grace given, free
the very sauntering flights of birds above the fronds of tight stalk curtain

ANGEL OF THE HOLY SPIRIT

Some calls him a double agent
but he knows no duplicity.
The Angel of the Holy Spirit, a scalpel,
cuts through flesh and spirit leaving no trace,
visits any recess, fills any abyss with an echo to decipher,
a mirror lends a reflection inverted, right for left, left for right,
spells Latin in the mysterious shape of a Cyrillic alphabet,
call and response to prayer,
Angel who reflects brilliance, in and out of itself
the nocturnal brightness in all and beyond constellations
put in its luminescent form—life even to the dead and untactile objects we
    deny
Angel versed in all the figures of the body, Love, the prosaic eroticism of
    human desires.
Of night and day, the dividing needle on the quadrant—every hour, time
    and eternity.
The angel of the Holy Spirit, a clever kleptomaniac returning all given
and taken with a godly hue of divine breath
riches in the pockets of your soul you did not know.

WEED ANGELS

Weeds in the yards,
equivocators of beauty, usurpers of flowers
aerial seeds of fallen angels,
dragons' teeth of wild rye plying underground
backbone of a tail every cut resuscitates for hundreds,
blue, seductive spring visitor, the spider wort
quick to divest itself spreading its infants for awaiting seasons
Shiso inoffensive nettles, little flag leaf of double-sided colors—
	green waving purple
a pleasure to the wind, minty, peppery and soon growing borders of its
	own.
Animal weeds of transfigured seeds—
sheep sorrel with no match but the shepherd's purse,
pigweed, chickweed to motherwort, lion's tail to the dandelions' bite
	rooting into the sidewalk
the spreading cat's claws over the fence climbing higher into a birch a brief
	yellow canopy
Oxalis showing out gracile false shamrocks over a basil pot,
bluebells pretending lavender blooms, wild chicory of intoxicating cobalt
	color
and the near-edible lamb's tongues bitter weeds of summer,
tare of cursed harvest mixing in triumphant poppies,
weeds at the gate pushing in under the fence like barbarians
disguised in false hopes of flowers that never come
pigweed made convivial as amaranth bending to the society garlic stale
	smell
monkey grass with virulent green tuffs
friends found foes, weeds of misconstrued intentions
rebellious greens dormant underground, free to the wind
fallen angels under the bird-bearing fig tree
the common rue in joyous golden florets redeeming itself, herb-of-grace.

WELL ANGEL

He flicks his eyes at the bottom
a glimpse of noon or moon
wet stones and luck of small maiden ferns.
Beyond the margin frogs call each other.
Thirst quencher, his halo rippling lips
when the bucket falls on his face
it gulps in his silvery water body
deeper than what you can pull out
the ring of a mirror—trembling and reappearing
the rope winches up, squeals to a stand-still.
The Well Angel shimmers in a glass,
expends through the water can over the geraniums,
angel of the gardener's hours,
the Well Angel
leveled eye,
ever silent and telluric
a life saver and giver
cool and profound,
good but for a nefarious poisoner—
carrions, herbicides, pesticides,
bad seasons holding him prisoner.

ANGEL'S HALO

After James Rosenquist's A Pale Angel's Halo

A bucket with a handle
hoop of a bent horizon to jump through
crew-cut grass
stubbles of blue
pale halo of angel plunging into yellow
the bucket, the bucket
sooner or later
you'll kick it.

ANGEL OF EPILOGUE

The angel of epilogue has slipped through the cover
wrung the space between every line
coursed back and forth every word from letter to letter.
He jumps back on the stage in a summersault of the plot,
more to it than Lot's wife turned into salt—
not to moralize, falsely conclude,
he holds his breath for a reversal
and lingers on the foretaste of a ripe fruit about to fall
not to end, relent or relapse.
The angel of epilogue returns to the folds of the living
companions an anonymous guy in a two-piece blue suit into a yellow cab
a commuter hinging her heels on a turnstile.
He considers whom the room may have hosted
with and without a view beyond the waves to see, a detour to the story
    line,
journeys, jaunts, forays, or escapades.
To the serendipity of a coin tossed, the angel of epilogue gives chance to
    evitability
the closing period on the page eyes follow in the margin of a down pillow
last word of a quill, the tip of an angel's finger.

JOGGING MONK

He treads along the woods and gravelly gravel roads
right after vigil, his Lectio Divina
fisted arms in balance and counterbalance
elbows swinging above hips, legs in binary motions
and deep breathing in and out, elevated torso,
foot tips bending heels up his canvas shoes
no panting, the rustle of his shirt in passing you by.
His way, gracile, almost sweatless
Jasmine, lilac strewn in his path overtaking fragrance.
His chosen name already taken, Jude,
he would have set for Judas, but not allowed, overloaded,
and took Juan, the Brother of the dark night into the night
jogger into the penumbra, Brother on the run
with no betrayal to his self-assigned miles.
Depth of the air inhaled, returned to the pneuma
God's touch through lungs and blood.
During the day the perfectionist worker,
silent disapprover of your head marking rhythm of chants at prayers
he goes into his running for ever as if to no return,
meek, humble and strong of heart past seventy,
He who takes your yoke and unburdens you.

BARBER BROTHER

A brown door and a covered transom window,
a chair, a swiveling stool, a shelf,
a room bright from a view opening to a live oak
a bare neon on the ceiling,
a crucifix on the wall opposite the mirror,
no confession room, the door reads Barber.
The monk, not tonsured, but bald on top
stands by the entry—almost obsequious
shiny clean, donning a white smock.
A former diplomat who harped on the Vatican,
strings of national interests, arpeggio negotiations, claws of intrigues,
he saw all what fell and fooled,
curls rolling at the snaps of clippers.
Eye level over the shelf he keeps Mary
an Icon of blond gold over a blue sky of a tilma,
a close-cropped Martin de Porres.
Queen Elizabeth over the dusty mantle
an air of subversion, faded smile of a religious flirtation.
The Pope faces her from across the hallway
as if the two could not believe to be so close.
He clips and at times steps back as if to recollect his job and older days,
the beaming heads of his brothers he sees from above.
He keeps a small tin box, beeswax,
shine and saintly smell for the monks' tonsured heads.

MONASTERY CROWS

The crows are faithful and poor in love.
Sleek in black almost blue
their beaks, prominent, to call and cut
they shriek in punctuations.
Solid coal over the tended green
each one to one for all
drawing invisible lines dividing the yard with their replies.
They love even if poor in love.
Unlike the rich and artsy
who spend their times from Winter residence to Summer residence
chasing the best in impatience,
crows inhabit the earth.
Black and bright in their plumage
if poor with a bit of grief under their wings
fix for a moment on a branch
they appear and disappear.
The abbot robed in black passing below
waving his hand makes no comparison to crow
by sent or sight
by rules or rights.
Telepathic, crows have their own demesne under God
none under the cloth and habit can ever know.
Returning pilgrims in lines they fly
riot in the belfry over the cloistered soul of the old abbot.

FLOWER BROTHER

Sunday, he emerges carrying blue Irises,
lilies, and Maiden ferns,
a few cabbage palm fronds,
sheers closing their silent beaks
the light just disclosed behind the river hill,
boxwood and red peeled trunks of crepe myrtles.
He picks and chooses, gathers them in his arms
he will push the iron gate and climb the serpentine brick path.
He pitched semi-pro baseball,
golfer, lifeguards, fencing master,
a life to the body, works of honed reflexes,
eyes of a blue cutting-edge, deft hands, perfect ambidextrous,
slant ball, whirled ball, knee ball. Hecatches all.
He embraces the flowers against his chest
and deposits them by the altar,
signs himself, arranges them in a white vase.
No ball to miss.
God and prayers, fragrant Easter between his two luminous hands.

COBBLER MONK

In the old days was the Cobbler Monk,
a puny, barrel-chested man—a Stentor voice uncontainable in his body.
His shop under the laundry stairs,
a small wooden bench, a sewing machine
with a see-through engine, belts, cogs, levers, long needle.
Soles, pairs against pairs, along a string
hanging there to find matching feet,
he would glue, hammer in with nails
sturdy and clamp to fit their master.
Cobbler Martin could refurbish the sore of a shoe
giving a pair a new life,
excoriating chafing places from any bunion,
smell of leather and oil,
families of shoestrings boxed by color and length.
What the cobbler, formerly discalced, couldn't do?
Known to the father—son proverbially wearing no shoes,
a belt maker, tongue puller to remanufacture galoshes,
a jimmy, lasting pliers, he can re-stich soles
pierce new eyes with his awl
no enmity for the new but what fits better to last
Brother Cobbler with pounce for shorthand
an extra mile to the thread worn monk straps
Crispin and Crispinian, saints faded and smeared,
a worn print over the bench.

NIGHTLY MONK

The nightly monk has two skies above his head
one of black burlap in a single pointed tip
the other, nocturnal, God's hand scattered stars and planets,
unveiled order he set to the great clock of *vitam eternam.*

Brother Stephen walks the cool slabs of the cloister
no side distraction to his eyes
small pupils, bright, under the shade of his hood
always going ahead, seeing in now and to the ever,

mechanical he makes and remakes his path
in thousands of thousands of steps since his postulancy
looking back would set him in reverse,
sin of memory,

nostalgia, the trick of the devil,
Lott's wife worth her weight of salt
for a glimpse of what her fate might have been.
All he sees from the funnel of his scapula

as in a long tunnel
dust of constellations
the Son of the sun and flecks from his cataract
his sight getting dimmer, his steps smaller and smaller

in diminishing increments
two by two in two till the end
infinitesimal to be one
with the one in and beyond the night.

HIDE AND SEEK

Because God is everywhere
Monks try to corner God to no avail
on earth and in heaven—
he knows no hiding but a lot of seeking,
no trick under his sleeves,
simple child's play as a rose bush
bending its flowers to the touch of wind
planted by a vineyard, it tells
mildew may come, or a pre-frost ascend the need of covering.

The immanence of God is irrefutable,
a trapezist of the Great Circus of the Air
in heaven to no limit of a tent
under all season somersaults of thunder
pirouette of lightning clearing the azure
on top of a steeple cross a rod
and a weathervane over the old farm refectory.
In seeking God under their capuches
Monks believe they know how to proceed,
be in the know of his moves
good graces of prayers
Vigil to Compline in processions.

God remains a mystery to our own eyes
a mystery in the remainder of all things
like the Spanish moss on oaks,
organ of light in blue and verdigris,
dark spine trunks and stigmata from fallen limbs
a dwelling place for spiders, squirrels, crows and cardinals
no snake, rats, possums can reach,
a cathedral of leaves, Mother wood of live oaks and love,
an everlasting canopy.

HUNGRY MONK

The hungry Brother is the one—whodunit—
came to the deserted refectory with cravings under his capuche,
taste of salt, infinite whiteness touching God.
From wave to wave, his watering mouth calls for
something tasty to appease, satisfy
only two eggs, dewy,
anonymous, cradled in the carton
he reaches for inside the fridge.
It is the world he wants to reconcile with a nocturnal appetite
and so, he lifts up the pan off the rack
as already engaged in an act of thievery,
the flames, a blue crown on the Vulcan top.
A bit of oil where he lets two suns cracked off the shells sizzle,
gently dropped from a secret life—whitening albumen, yolks rounding
soon to burst to satiety—had he his way
Devil's eggs,
the abbot would call the Grand Inquisitor, the Bishop
he leaves it at that mystery, sunny side-up, S & P,
for the ogling Brother Chef who daily counts the eggs.

DRAGONFLIES

You sat at the table in the mildewed garden chair
fallen Spanish moss grow on its back.
In the early-rise of the hour the whole world takes a vacation from itself,
insects at rest, roaches ceasing to run their gravitational circuses,
mosquitoes heavenly gone to zero buzzing at your ears.
You notice the dragonflies, silver, green,
   blue, dual wings of glistening cellophane
small notes that will soon take off the musical score of disused cloth lines,
and the incinerator will start burning the weekly garbage.

In the chapel, the red head Scola director with blue streaked hair
her voice so high no thunder can catch—
blend in, lead on, follow each other she instructs.
Put lightness and spiritedness—fawns gamboling over meadows.

Forget the score, think something light and lifting she says.
A cold beer one Brother says
a glass of bubbly in sunlight,
snow plumes behind a skier another continues,
the small lift up jumping off a cargo plane,
the parachute opens releasing adrenaline
the sky in one brief red poppy bloom of fabric,
the dragonflies seep dew over a cloth line
all lifting up, giddy, to nowhere you know—ephemeral, light in light.

GOD IS HERE 24/ 7

Monks circle him in prayers and canticles,
all surrender, white flag robes, albs.

Vigil to vesper, the candles lit giving presence to the air,
yellow, orange, briefly blue pupils of flames.

When it rains hard over the back chapel
buckets collect the present time given to eternity
Him, and the mother of all—visible and invisible,
ripples to tic-toc of drops follow—swift or slow, with no end and
    beginning.

To listen to God hear beyond your ears and heart
behind what is given to your eyes.

A novice comes and empties the buckets—
not everything is holy—but water—present or absent a part of all things.

The sun has come back and wasps madder than ever,
they devour the blue, cloy wisterias flowers.

Twigs and brambles Brother Vincent crushes over the narrow path along
    the bluff
a last turn opens to a promontory over the gray green river.
Below the current has nooked empty plastic bottles, rebukes, torn
    fishlines.

God has tired him—he would like a break
a breath to catch over the unslept hours,
    regain the pneuma of his soul floating over prayers,
a little gap—an interstice in the totality of the totality of the maker,
evil would it be in an absence of good?
Unsatisfied appetite for the riverbank dawn
rising in dew to the fullness of his bearded mouth and taste.

CALL TO NO ANSWER

In the baseball end field behind the monastery
monks play an old game of pelota,
how they fly clouds of white,
sleeves rolled to collapsible angels' wings
who to tell the orb of a ball
to conjecture its curvature
just to put your palm behind your head with no touching
the sentient eye behind your back of your body tells where it is,
in crossword puzzle of God, no proof and refutation
a ladybug crawls over the hands of Lady of Lourdes
an incarnadine moving mole.
What a lover awaits in the predication of the beloved
a grammar of risk and revelation, copula, cesura.
Always tomorrow the fortune teller murmurs closing shop,
still a fortune to mine in the conjunctions of yesterdays.
A single blue jay has taken dominion of the cloth line
the rabbit furtive with one ear to the moon, one ear toward the ground
all where to jump in between—
the eyes of a caboose approaching in the rewinding of a film
as memories die and revive
you paddle the lake across
dripping of the motioning oars,
closing and opening,
the rain will soon confound under the domain of a solid sky.

FAWNS

Two fawns have come,
deep breathing heard
heaving one after the other, syncopation,
emerge from the edge of water,
into the green clearing
a path only they can take
early into day as a canticle at a cusp of light.
They stop and stoop, lift up their heads, clear-eyed
gamboling of a fresh day they own in their survey
and you, made invisible, turned into a naught.
The first creaking of your shoes will take them away.
Lean, muscular, chestnut fur
they stand on holy ground of the sleepy vigil,
and forbidding, your mind has already seized them
into the hunter's sight from peace to blood
from intelligent eyes to the blotting nuzzle of a gun,
instinct or folly, to possess, and obliterate.

CANCER MONK

In memory of Chef Sammy

Oncologists in Japan train dogs to discern cancer by smell
most birds are devoid of olfactory perceptions
the titmouse, tufted, doodling its head to smell berries and sweetness
suffering, happiness, we endow animals with their perceptions.
How does a dry cough catch the rattling of bones
near hollow of the thoracic cage, little beads of blood smeared in a
    kerchief.
In medicine, all lies bellow the decimal point,
   the mass of the body measures its perishability
in alchemy, the belief follows the degree of the moon,
   a hair crossed by dusk and stars.
Acedia, a manifestation of discontent
autoimmune of the soul as the Brother shuffling in his cell to the empty
    refectory
his feet like chopsticks refuse to bend
no miracle to engage the stiffness of ankylosis
an anxiety of not loving women,
   a false virtue, rotten plum, to attract and mask fears?
At night he takes to the forest with the same dream
the oaks with cicatrices, the pines of corrugated lip-eyes
the elongated vulvas on ash trees, birch shedding silver rings and bracelets
and mad he tossed himself to the ground till he finds himself naked on a
    bare hill
then he prays for the dying and the sick
all cloths of fear shed he is one of them.

DEPARTED

The Brothers gone from the congregation of the night
the Cooper River, a stream of small noises—turtles, frogs,
a current the coming sun deliberates—
the old metal bridge hiccupping planks a truck crosses
Men of Chants—portal of vespers into day.
God has long hunched his ways through Strawberry Field Landing
Moon gone from his eyes, the keeper, Old Georges slow wheels the gate
   open.
Is prayer a contraption of our wishing minds through air and whispers?
By the Post Road a car, driver's door ajar, lights on
in a standstill suspended against the black top, crickets' din
the lining live oaks doubling their darkness in the 4 am night
the car perimetered by its metal shell
as if alone, an object encapsulated into an atmosphere of its own
the ceiling light an aura, someone slumped over the wheel.
He already knows, he will walk all the way
call emergency, give details.
The woman whose heart gave to God,
stopped before she could go beyond the gate
light will soon dissipate her way, merge into the day,
he left to explain all,
facts, details, time—his, hers, God's.
At the far end of the alley
two does cross and look to the headlights and then away, away.

LEARNING GOD

For Rachel

You left the Monks
their regular count of hours, tangent of sky and chant,
not to forget, some petty habits,
the distance—what to put up and test humility,
foot after foot like a rosary beading along the cloistered walk
for God knows what, and you don't.
The place in the city you retrieved boxes out, boxes in.
The word rictus you had to check.

How she, love and beloved,
described her face, re-imaging out of Bell Palsy—
childhood photos, over fifty years old,
black and white, some photocopied to greater contrast
featured lines underlined,
pig tails and the same double half-moon of her lips orbicularis oris.
Risorus yet not flagging—Summer snow cone from a straw she sips
uncannily reveals a smile.

How do we find placidity, expression—by God,
dimple's Grace, risorus, a mantra, the elect triggers the right lip
    movements.
The little map your mind draws, muscles and emotions,
mind's memory and kinesis in a tug of war,
what the mirror served your eyes exercised.
God to love, you wanted a whole embrace,
food of the bitter taste, your chin tensed mentalis,
bread your tongue long salivates to release peace and appease.
Zygomatic you consciously paralleled.
a facial twitch your eye circled, your brain zeroed on
as what may be the first human effort
extract a sound toward a word,
God granted and gave you to relearn.

SHOE LEGACY

In the hierarchy of the livings
shoes take the inner imprints,
stake the ground,
sand, mud, concrete,
grass, tarmac, piers, marble stairs, board walks.
Crampons of conquerors and hikers,
pas-de-chat in stilettoes, eye hole of a beggar's
the wading gaiters of the anglers
and dust for the barefooted,
the peaceful disapprover shaking sands off his sandals,
in the horror of winter war, an infantry man tearing off iced toes with his
    shoes,
Victor Frankl confesses in his journal swapping a better pair with a
    cadaver in Dachau,
the long worn and weary ones making memory that talks in Van Gogh's
    bodkins,
history attests the dictator's wife, Imelda, had a museum full
for several lives to wear in a country of barefoot people.
angels it is known wear none.

"OUR CHILDREN ARE EXPLOSIVE"*

*After reading the article, 'Please Save My Live.' A Bomb
Specialist Defuses Explosives Strapped to Children.***

In the work of the Devil
not-so-to-speak, all literal,
a walking bomb.
One twelve-year-old girl,
belly pregnant of nails and shrapnel
bomb strapped for death delivery.
One of an army of children
the ordnance team sergeant declares,
a work of life and death
not only skill,
courage and competence,
a short prayer between diffuser and human carrier.

She walked and trudged for two days
longer wait than the market shopping
her place of final sacrifice,
insanity in her, insanity out of her,
the Mufti who gave her Allah 's blessing
and plugged in the pair of wires.
Should the two held in a rubber hose touch
a brief kiss of death into eternity.

She unveiled her face
peeling off the black fabric between thumb and forefinger
over her abused innocence.
Scissors, carpet cutter
the sergeant carves out her delivery from her belly
a weight of death that sags to her knees,

* Title borrowed from a poem by Robert Priest in *Reading the Bible by Backwards*
(2008).

** by Joe Parkinson and Drew Hinshaw, *The Wall Street Journal*, July 26, 2019.

50/50, he collects carefully in a bag
her aborted parcel,
a Coke and a smile.

ASHES

For my brothers

La ceniza es el humo que se deja tocar
el fuego ya de luto por si mismo*

Antonio Pacheco, *La Ceniza*

Three sons, we came to the river
the river that draws its name in its passage,
sonorous and sleek under a bridge
to a near silence of its turning
further ahead by a storm-splintered oak.

We dispersed ashes, thin and lean as water sprays,
bluish, silver flakes wind strewn and absorbed.
A half pound of father's out of a bag, lighter than flour.

The three of us on foot, we came to the river
mixing mothers with fathers, gone,
from another half-pound bag
spring wheat light into the waters.

The river that is mother's and father's,
each, both and none.
An empty paper sachet we crumpled and tossed,
a white crown given to the stream
hesitating, swaying, and then with a nod drifting away,
ashes with no sackcloth
the river dissipates to light
particles penance free.

* "The ash is the smoke that can be touched
the fire already in mourning for itself"

PASSED AWAY

Just your fingertip between the glass tabletop and its frame
no cut, no bruise
a pinch leaving a black comma of blood under your skin.
You were rummaging in your father's office, recently passed away
still full of the living man
and all that fits into files, name-tagged, and alphabetized
tallies and memorandum in letters, bills, loans, installments
by years, by days, by hours, by the end of the minute you just breathed in.
An olivewood rosary you pulled out of a file cabinet spilled
a brief, watery rustling
the prayers all scattered on the floor
the lean cross alone hanging down a string.
If a rosary is a circular path
with a ladder to an ancient encyclical chant
the barren cross between your thumb and index
Jacob's last rung passing into high heaven.

INTO THE GREAT SILENCE

The movie screen stretched across the porch
you showed a film about the silence of the monks
almost silent to the silent between the bells
and a few night birds behind the oleander.
Darkness grew colder around us, and I served tea
the little sips of breathing while a monk took a new habit
the tailor brother measuring the novice, triple-fold garments
where he will grow from within, shiver and shrivel from without
God and what not God—cantata and breath within each body
from their lungs to the keystone.
Easter's snow where in pairs they will climb the long syncline
and glide down, giddy, white against white as the film shows
to the same color of the screen,
a page given to the echo of God.

Acknowledgements

Many thanks to the following magazines that first published these poems:

"Hide and Seek," "Angel of Frost" in *Briar Cliff Review*; "Angel of Rope," in *The Cape Rock*; "Jogging Monk," in *Christian Century*; "Angel of Metal" in Hampden-Sydney Poetry Review; "Angels of Visions" in *South Carolina Review*; "Ashes," *Louisiana Literature*; "Exterminating Angel," and "Roadside Angels" in *Valley Voices*; "Angel's Line," in *Vallum*.

Thank you to the Virginia Center for the Creative Arts and Piccolo Spoleto Festival for a fellowship allowing me to have time and leisure to work on this manuscript and discuss some of the poems included in this collection with fellows.

A generous stipend from the Mississippi Department of Employment Security contributed to the making of this manuscript.